SNOOPY

features as

The Winter Wonder Dog

Charles M. Schulz

PEANUTS is a registered trademark of
United Feature Syndicate, Inc.
Based on the PEANUTS® comic strip
by Charles M. Schulz.

Originally published in 1988 as 'Snoopy Stars as the
Terror of the Ice'.
This edition published in 2002 by Ravette Publishing.

Printed and bound in Great Britain
for Ravette Publishing Limited,
Unit 3, Tristar Centre,
Star Road, Partridge Green,
West Sussex RH13 8RA
by Cox & Wyman, Berkshire.

ISBN: 1 84161 163 8

PEANUTS

12-9

SCHULZ

© 1977 United Feature Syndicate, Inc.

© 1977 United Feature Syndicate, Inc.

AS LONG AS WE'RE JUST PRACTICING, I HAVE A SUGGESTION

MAYBE YOU SHOULD SHOOT AT THE OTHER GOAL FOR A WHILE...

12-27

1-25 © 1983 United Feature Syndicate, Inc.

Other PEANUTS titles published by Ravette ...

Pocket Books	ISBN	Price
Man's Best Friend	1 84161 066 6	£2.99
Master of Disguise	1 84161 161 1	£2.99
Master of the Fairways	1 84161 067 4	£2.99
The Fearless Leader	1 84161 104 2	£2.99
The Fitness Fanatic	1 84161 029 1	£2.99
The Flying Ace	1 84161 027 5	£2.99
The Great Entertainer	1 84161 160 3	£2.99
The Great Philosopher	1 84161 064 X	£2.99
The Legal Beagle	1 84161 065 8	£2.99
The Literary Ace	1 84161 026 7	£2.99
The Master Chef	1 84161 107 7	£2.99
The Matchmaker	1 84161 028 3	£2.99
The Music Lover	1 84161 106 9	£2.99
The Sportsman	1 84161 105 0	£2.99
The Tennis Ace	1 84161 162 X	£2.99
Little Books		
Charlie Brown - Friendship	1 84161 156 5	£2.50
Charlie Brown - Wisdom	1 84161 099 2	£2.50
Educating Peanuts	1 84161 158 1	£2.50
Lucy - Advice	1 84161 101 8	£2.50
Peanuts - Life	1 84161 157 3	£2.50
Peppermint Patty - Blunders	1 84161 102 6	£2.50
Snoopy - Laughter	1 84161 100 X	£2.50
Snoopy - Style	1 84161 155 7	£2.50
Colour Landscapes		
Passion for Peanuts	1 84161 153 0	£4.50
Snoopy Unleashed	1 84161 154 9	£4.50
Miscellaneous		
Peanuts Anniversary Treasury	1 84161 021 6	£9.99
Peanuts Treasury	1 84161 043 7	£9.99
You Really Don't Look 50 Charlie Brown	1 84161 020 8	£7.99

All PEANUTS books are available at your local bookshop or from the publisher at the address below. Just tick the titles required and send the form with your payment to:-

RAVETTE PUBLISHING, Unit 3, Tristar Centre, Star Road, Partridge Green, West Sussex RH13 8RA

Prices and availability are subject to change without prior notice.

Please enclose a cheque or postal order made payable to **Ravette Publishing** to the value of the cover price of the book and allow the following for UK postage and packing:-

55p for the first book + 30p for each additional book, except *You Really Don't Look 50 Charlie Brown* when please add £1.50 p&p per copy and the two *Treasuries* when please add £2.50 p&p per book.

Name ....

Address ....

....

....